6 stories
for:

....

6 Stories
every Mom
should tell

Denise J. Hughes

HARVEST HOUSE PUBLISHERS

EUGENE, OREGON

Scripture quotations are taken from

The Holy Bible, New International Version®, NIV®. Copyright © 1973, 1978, 1984, 2011 by Biblica, Inc.® Used by permission. All rights reserved worldwide.

The Holy Bible, New Living Translation, copyright ©1996, 2004, 2007, 2013 by Tyndale House Foundation. Used by permission of Tyndale House Publishers, Inc., Carol Stream, Illinois 60188. All rights reserved.

The New American Standard Bible®, © 1960, 1962, 1963, 1968, 1971, 1972, 1973, 1975, 1977, 1995 by The Lockman Foundation. Used by permission. (www.Lockman.org)

The New King James Version®. Copyright © 1982 by Thomas Nelson, Inc. Used by permission. All rights reserved.

Interior design by Janelle Coury

Cover design by Connie Gabbert Design + Illustration

Published in association with the literary agency of the Steve Laube Agency, LLC, 24 W. Camelback Rd. A-635, Phoenix, Arizona 85013.

6 STORIES EVERY MOM SHOULD TELL
Copyright © 2018 by Denise J. Hughes
Published by Harvest House Publishers
Eugene, Oregon 97402
www.harvesthousepublishers.com

ISBN 978-0-7369-6818-8

Printed in China

17 18 19 20 21 22 23 24 25 26 / RDS-JC / 10 9 8 7 6 5 4 3 2 1

6 stories every mom should tell

I take my seat on the top row of metal bleachers and peer across the football field. The high school band plays the familiar "Pomp and Circumstance" as the graduates begin their procession. They're wearing identical caps and gowns, so I strain to find the one I'm here for. The one who made me a mom eighteen years ago. The one I stayed home with. Every day. Year after year. The one I taught to read. The one I taught to swim. The one I drove to piano lessons and theater rehearsals and youth group.

The one who is about to leave for college. *In another state.*

Along the edge of the field, the breeze pulls the green and white balloons in one direction. That's how I feel as a mom. Every instinct inside me wants to pull in one direction. I want to preserve each moment and resist this onward march toward the future. Yet, I also want to embrace this new season the way an artist enjoys a new palette of colors to paint with. It's with this curious mix of joy-for-the-future and nostalgia-for-the-past that I've been doing a lot of reflecting lately.

From this mom-heart place of looking back and looking ahead, I've realized six of the most important stories I want my children to know. They're stories that happened when my kids were either too young to remember or perhaps not yet born. They're stories I've taken for granted and assumed my kids already knew. They're six stories every mom should tell.

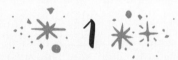

Tell the Story of Their Birth

I recently wrote the birth story of my oldest child. When my daughter read it, she commented on the parts she'd never heard before. Her words surprised me. I assumed she knew all those details. So we shared a long chat over mint tea as I told her more about the day she was born. Our conversation reminded me of the importance of telling our kids the story of their birth.

If you've adopted children, tell the story of how God brought them into your lives. Nothing in all creation is more beautiful than an adoption story, for it echoes God's heart and the way He has adopted us as His children (see Ephesians 1:4-5).

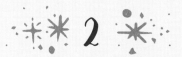

Tell the Story of How You Picked Their Name

Proverbs 22:1 says, "A good name is more desirable than great riches" (NIV). What process did you go through when you chose your child's name? Did you pick a name that carries part of your family's history? Did you select a name that reflects a truth or a person in Scripture? Tell the story of how you picked your child's name.

3

Tell a Story That Reflects
Their Strengths

From the moment a child is born, parents observe certain characteristics in their kids. Hebrews 11:23 says, "Moses' parents hid him [from Pharaoh] for three months after he was born, because they saw he was no ordinary child" (NIV). What stories can you recall—of your children when they were young—that clearly point to their strengths?

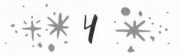

4

Tell the Story of How You Met Jesus

Of all the stories we could tell, this is the most important one. After reading Bible stories together, let's also tell the story of how we met Jesus. Let's talk about the way Jesus continues to transform us into His image a little more each day.

5

Tell the Story of How You Met Their Dad

As husband and wife, we live our story every day. We know the events that brought us together, but our kids need to hear this story too. One of the ways we can honor our spouse and express unity as a couple is to celebrate with our kids the story of how we came together.

I understand that not every story comes straight out of a Disney movie. Many of us have experienced the pain of broken stories. But when we surrender our brokenness to Christ, our lives become stories of redemption and hope. Share the story of how you met your child's father, and how your child is the most beautiful blessing to come from that union.

Tell the Story of Your Dreams

When our children are young, it's hard for them to imagine that we actually once lived before they were born. It's like the teacher who meets one of her students in the grocery store. The student is surprised to discover that her teacher exists outside the classroom. In the same way, our children might be surprised to learn we once dreamed of being an astronaut or a veterinarian. Share your dreams with your kids—dreams both past and present.

At the end of the graduation ceremony, the seniors move their tassels from the right side of their caps to the left in a symbolic gesture of completion. If I had a tassel of my own, I would move it too. Because, in a way, I've also graduated—into a new season of motherhood.

I watch as my daughter and her friends toss their white caps into the air, and I breathe another prayer, placing these past eighteen years into the hands of Him who loves her even more than I do. Then I recall each story I've told her, knowing she takes these stories with her everywhere she goes.

Mom, have you told these stories to your kids? Have you written any of them down? I invite you to write them here, in this book, and then give them to your children.

Son or Daughter, I invite you to treasure these stories right from your mom's heart.

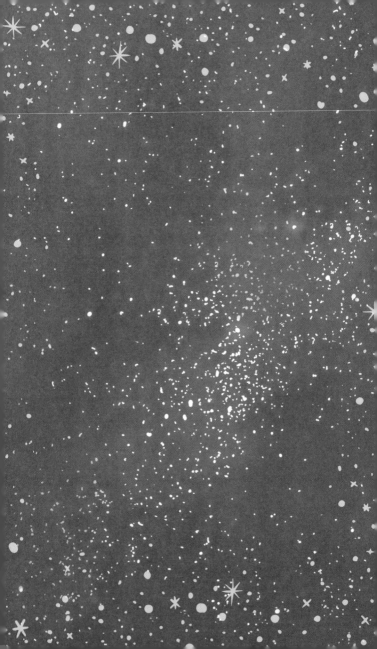

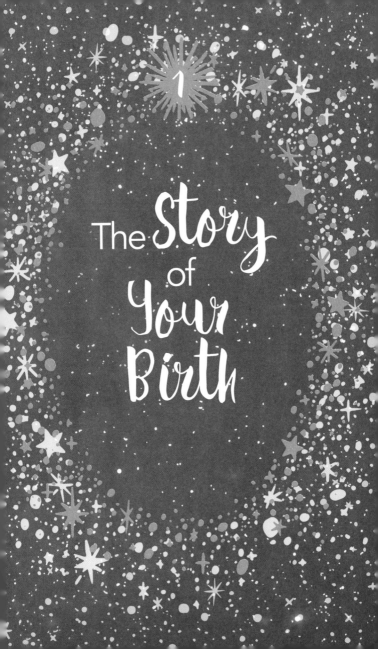

1

The Story
of
Your
Birth

For this child I prayed, and the LORD has granted me my petition which I asked of Him.

1 SAMUEL 1:27 NKJV

The littlest feet
make the
biggest footprints
in our hearts.

AUTHOR UNKNOWN

Behold, children are
a gift of the LORD,
the fruit of the womb
is a reward.

PSALM 127:3 NASB

2

How I
Picked
Your
Name

A good name is
more desirable than
great riches;
to be esteemed is better
than silver or gold.

PROVERBS 22:1 NIV

I will give you treasures
hidden in the darkness—
secret riches. I will do
this so you may know
that I am the LORD,
the God of Israel,
the one who calls you
by name.

ISAIAH 45:3 NLT

Do not fear,
for I have redeemed you;
I have called you
by name;
you are Mine!

ISAIAH 43:1 NASB

3

A Story
That
Reflects
Your
Strengths

The Lord is
my strength and shield.
I trust him with
all my heart.
He helps me, and my heart
is filled with joy.

PSALM 28:7 NLT

Be sure you put your feet
in the right place,
and then stand firm.

ABRAHAM LINCOLN

It is God who arms me
with strength and
keeps my way secure.

PSALM 18:32 NIV

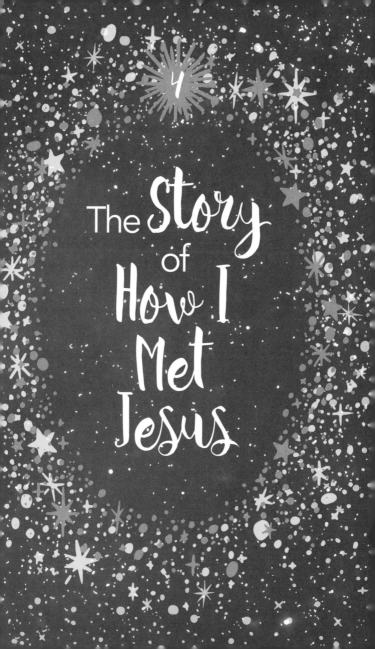

4

The Story
of
How I
Met
Jesus

You also were included
in Christ when you heard
the message of truth,
the gospel of your salvation.

EPHESIANS 1:13 NIV

To all who
did receive him,
to those who
believed in his name,
he gave the right to become
children of God.

JOHN 1:12 NIV

The Lord
—who is the Spirit—
makes us more and more
like him as we are changed
into his glorious image.

2 CORINTHIANS 3:18 NLT

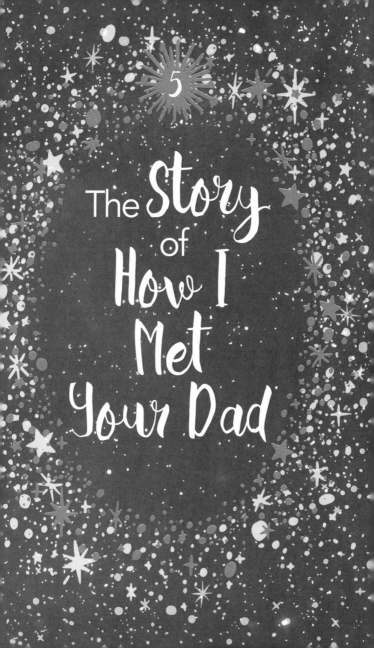

5

The Story
of
How I
Met
Your Dad

Now these three remain:
faith, hope and love.
But the greatest
of these is love.

1 CORINTHIANS 13:13 NIV

Dear friends,
let us love one another,
for love comes from God.

1 JOHN 4:7 NIV

Greater love
has no one than this:
to lay down one's life
for one's friend.

JOHN 15:13 NIV

6

The Story
of
My Dreams

Take delight in the LORD,
and he will give you
the desires of your heart.

PSALM 37:4 NIV

A mother is
someone who dreams
great dreams for you,
but then she lets you chase
the dreams you have for
yourself and loves you
just the same.

AUTHOR UNKNOWN

Commit to the LORD
whatever you do,
and he will establish
your plans.

PROVERBS 16:3 NIV

I remember
my mother's prayers,
and they have always
followed me.
They have clung to me
all my life.

ABRAHAM LINCOLN